The Rain Reinvented Me

Contents

Part 1:
Pain
You
Societal diseases

Part 2:
Humanity
Hope
Love
Joy

Part 1

All I can see is rain

Pain

I remember as a child when I used to chant,
"Rain, rain, go away, come again another day!"
Now the words have changed;
My mind is more deranged
And it begins to say,
"Pain, pain, go away, come again another day."

They asked
"What scares you little child?"
She told them to guess
And so, they did:

Are you afraid of the dark?

Walking alone to the park?

Watching horror shows?

Not knowing where to go?

Being followed home?

Being outcasted?

Slenderman?

The monsters under your bed?

She said "all except for the last one. The monsters aren't under my bed...they're inside my head."

Happy.
It's a word that is used ever so often
But I wonder,
What does it truly mean to be happy?
Because I don't think it means fake laughs and smiles.
I don't think it means barely surpassing these trials
And forgetting who you truly are in the midst of all this madness.

Some find happiness when watching a new movie or when getting a new outfit,
Others find happiness in the harm brought to them for all of eternity.
Maybe not happiness,
But it's surely their serenity.

I won't find happiness,
Leave me be
Let me weep
And let me fall sleep.
Let my tears glisten under the moon's bright gaze
And let my heart drop once again.
Let me simply remain,
In the dust that makes me human.

Numbness is a disease that controls me;
I try to cure it but a laugh, a good mark, and compliments don't seem to be the remedy.
When they say something 'funny' I don't laugh because it hurts too much.
A smile on my face takes so much effort but they just don't understand.
My eyes scream for help, but no one answers.

You yell at me
And as you do so
You ask,
"Is this funny?
If not then...why do you laugh when you are clearly in trouble?"
Oh dear yeller,
I laugh for a simple reason:
To keep my mouth from running
And yelling back.
You'd love my laugh a lot more
If you knew what words could be said.

Why am I smiling you ask?
What could possibly make me happy in this moment?
And to this I answer:
Absolutely nothing.
Nothing makes me happy,
Nothing at all.
I'm simply smiling to keep it all in;
To hide the truths
That haunt me from within.

People always tell me that I should try to be happy.
Put a smile on your face,
It's as simple as that.
Put a smile on your face to hide your pain;
To make life easier for the people around you
Because they won't have to deal with your problems.
The ones that cause your inner turmoil
And your sadness
And your agony.
The pain they see when your true self is revealed.
So they tell you to be happy
As a way out.
They tell you to be happy but wearing a smile simply isn't enough.

There is a kind of anger that controls me.
I don't understand what it is.
What necessarily caused it?
What is the root for all of this?
It's pure madness.
It comes and goes as it pleases,
It leaves my head aching
And my hands shaking.
I want to break something,
The wall
The desk
The glass
My hand.
Anything that will make this feeling go away.
Please, if anything, don't let it stay.
I just want to hideaway,
But not even that can be my escape.

How can I feel at ease and happy again?
I'll just lower my gaze and write with my pen.
How do I settle down the rebel in me?
I honestly just want to feel peace and serenity.
How do I regain motivation
When everything around me seems to have no solution?

I feel nothing but emptiness as the ink hits the page,
I lie awake tonight,
My head aches;
Mainly from the thoughts that I process.
I need to feel something;
Anything at this point.
The clock is ticking;
There's nothing to rejoice.
So, I'll write words then scribble them out
And put this process on repeat
Until my ink runs out.

If she goes on a plane
Will her sorrows leave her?
Will her pain fly away too?
Will the bright sun that is thousands of feet
closer than it was when she was on the ground
come and dry her off?
Or will a cloud reappear,
Blocking her from the sun's gaze?
Will the sun ever be able to
Dry the rain away?

We've all been hurt before,
Some more than others.
Our battles are violent and angry smothers
across our brain.
Our minds are awake, we can no longer
sleep with ease.
We think that our fates will mimic these
terrible memories.
We feel as though we are trapped under the
sea.
Running out of air, we can no longer
breathe.
Our lungs grasp at any oxygen that they can
get,
But we're beginning to feel brain dead.

Closed doors hide things,
Things that I can't even begin to explain.
They hide secrets of sadness.
Secrets of loss.
Secrets of sanity
And a lack thereof.
Closed doors hide my fears
And my everyday truths;
They hide what my eyes have been forced to see,
They make invisible to you what is all too clear to me.

I didn't know that being this way would keep me up in my bed,
I just thought that after the tears swelled my eyes and burned my cheeks,
Perhaps my mind would be at ease.
But it's not, so I lie awake staring at the ceiling,
My mind is blank.
My thoughts are empty.
My soul is vanishing into the darkness of eternity.

I lie, I seem to do it all the time.
When I'm panicking inside, and the horror on my face shows, and people ask if I'm ok, I'll reply that I'm doing just fine
And I try, every single day, to not make it a lie
But lies can be an addiction.
When you want something so badly sometimes you'll move into desperation mode and will lie.
You don't have it.
You don't have what you want, what you need,
Which is
Peace and mental serenity.
But as long as they see what you want them to
And you keep your tears for the pillow
You'll be fine, simply because no one will know
That my smile keeps my tears from falling
And "I'm fine" will keep me from balling
So, I'll continue to lie,
Because I'm fine.

Sometimes a certain smell will take me back
to when I was young,
It usually reminds me of the foods cooked
by my mum.
She would remind us about how everything
really mattered,
And about how one day we would miss our
youth that was shattered.

I remember sitting near the windowsill
staring into the darkness of the night,
Thoughts begin to cloud my mind:
I need to leave this place, I need to escape
from here tonight.

I think one day I might just leave this place,
But if I do I'm scared I'll be labelled a
disgrace,
A disappointment,
Late to that appointment.
Negative thoughts still circling through my
head,
I'm just waiting until I can finally go to bed.

But then I remember, there really is no
escape.
The ghosts and ghouls in my head just get
stronger.
Dream format,
Simply laying flat.
Unable to move, to choose, to think, to
control.
Left to sleep with my monsters in the dark,
All alone.

You.

This deafening silence hurts too much
I can't stand here much longer,
It feels like my chest will be crushed.
I feel like if I stay with you,
I might just die.
So my heart is pounding
And my mind is racing
I feel like screaming
But there's no escaping
The dark reality,
The dark truth,
There is simply no escaping people like you.

You took me in
When I was low,
When I was lost,
And had no place to go.

You had the perfect timing,
Was it by plan or pure choice?
You had it and you tried to save my voice.

But then one day I noticed things changed,
It wasn't innocent or sweet anymore,
You wanted more
And you left me torn.

When I see you in the day
And you creep up in the night
I can't help but wonder
What your true intentions are for tonight.

He wondered why she did not laugh like she used to

Or smile

Or sing

He wondered, as if it wasn't his fault.

He knew it was but could not bare taking the blame for the breaking of such a beautiful heart.

Traitors.
They left me
Stranded here
In a cage all alone
I'm locked in by their petty lies
And my own vulnerable truths.
By what I have entrusted them with.
I trusted too much
And I loved too hard
So much so that I accidentally locked myself up
With the key thrown away.
The bittersweet truth
Is that I'd rather be abandoned by those who give me fake love
Then continue to love those who do nothing but talk.

I told you so much,
My heart was crushed.
I trusted you in my times of need.
I told you my worries
And of my future plans
We talked
And laughed together
I couldn't see through you, at that time.

I gave you so much love
And I defended you when
People were talking their same old talk.
I was there for you
When you said you were hurt
So how is it that I'm the one who's in the wrong?
Yea that's fine,
Because now you're just stranded here all alone.

My mind is a garden
Filled with flowers to the brim.
The blue ones represent grace
The yellow represent kindness
The pink ones represent faith
And the red ones represent no more falling for your tricks.
You got the best of me this time
But I promise you
That even though you think I need you
And even though you think that I'm desperate and all alone
That I will never
Bow down to someone's evil throne.

You think you helped me so much

So you keep on pointing out every time that I was sad and I ranted
But I hope you don't forget all those restless nights I spent
Talking with you about your own problems.

I'll admit that I was naïve, but then again,
I thought that I could trust you.
I thought you were different from the crowd.
Thought I could stay here;
Never knew you'd make me frown.
Because I've been hurt
And I've been left
And I've been alone
But I never thought you'd be the one
To leave me
Here.
I just have to say
Thank the lord that you're gone
Because, little girl,
I draw the line at fake.

A broken heart doesn't only mean that a lover tore it apart.
It means that someone who you put so much time and effort into was disloyal.
They hurt you;
They betrayed you.
People can betray you so you mustn't rely
On anyone
Especially those who only think for themselves
Because in the end,
To them you aren't special.
They don't care about your heart,
Or your head.
So you mustn't rely on anyone
Because in this big world it seems to be every person for themselves.

You call me lazy
Straight to my face
And you say I lack commitment
Because I'm leaving so I've lost all wanting to be here
And that I no longer care
But I mean to be honest,
I really don't.
I don't care.
But,
It's not because I'm leaving.
You see,
I've been this way all along
You choose to label it
As a means of my way out
You decide to tell me
Who I am
And what this situation is about
But you lack the basic knowledge
Surrounding my very health
And so you assume
Things about me because some things simply cannot be explained
You choose who I am
Without even knowing my true name.

You're so damn confusing,
You make me cry at night.
I'm still waiting for your replies, for that quick follow back.
I guess I'm not worth it.

Your face tells lies.
Your eyes are so mysterious, they keep on reeling me in.
But you make me feel like a lunatic, like I can't ever win.
You keep on sending mixed signals,
One moment you notice my existence,
The next we walk through the distance
But you don't even look in my direction.
We feel each others presence
But you still make me feel nonexistent.

I saw you
And I told myself I can't.
I can't go for you.
I have to stay focused;
I have to win
And falling for you would get in the middle of my plans but
Who could resist
The sweetest smile
And the purest laugh?
Eventually I'd wished that we'd have a love that would last.
But then one day everything changed
I thought you felt this way about me too
But I was clearly wrong
I was just a fool all along.
Searching for gold
And all I found was a fraud
Fools gold is all I loved
But I still felt rich with it in my crown.

He reeled her in
With his beautiful lies
Spewed sweet words at her
From left to right
And so she was bent back and forth by his sweet talk
She slowly started falling
More and more.
She had been attention deprived
And he knew exactly what he would have to give her
To try to control
A mind that was not very free
From constant worry, loneliness, and misery.
He made her feel free but in reality she was nothing more than his toy

And when boys are bored of playing with the same old toys they move on to the next;

They act as if you never existed.

Love feels like a drug.
I crave it,
I wait for it,
It feels like I can't live without it.
But even the thing I can't live without
Is slowly killing me;
Is taking my heart and ripping it into 3.

Love is like a drug.
You're reeled in and then you're its slave.
You work hard for it day by day,
But it's slowly taking you away.
Your conscience mind and soul
Are no longer kept safe
You're all alone
With your drug
Craving even more
Day by day,
Slowly dying away.

You said you loved her
From left to right
Up and down
And in between.
That you loved her smell,
And to caress her cheeks.
You loved her sincerity,
And the way her shoes would squeak.
You said you loved her,
So why did you hurt her?
Why did you leave her with nothing?
Left her to rot.
You left her for another.
Left even after you said you'd always love each other.

Last year everything was different.
You weren't so awkward around me,
You were accepting and kind
I thought that was who you were but I was clearly blind.
I might miss those countless hours on the phone with you
But I do not miss your treacherous personality
The one that only followed the crowd,
Didn't like being different; was a coward.
Although we talk it's not how we used to
But that's ok, I'm the one who left you anyway.

I try so hard to keep afloat,
To not drown in this sinking boat.
But I feel as though there are weights pulling me down.
You tied them onto me
And watched me sink
You didn't even stop to think,
Or maybe you did but didn't really care.
I mean, what can you do? Life's just not fair.
I'm still confused as to why it was you,
You knew all the pain I was already going through.
Yet you still betrayed me
You left me torn
My skin had raw cuts and you added salt to the wounds.
I thought I could trust you.
My heart was worn,
And you pricked it like a thorn.

Societal Diseases

In the midst of the madness called life,
I wonder if I can truly surrender.
If my words can ever enter the heart,
 Allowing for it to render.
If one day I can look up at the sky
And just keep wondering what stories it holds.
If I can keep concentrated as I write that test
Or as I watch the new story unfold.

I wonder in the midst of this madness,
If I fail just one more time,
Can I get up again
And win at my final try?
Can I look at the direction that the wind blows and claim what's there as mine?
Can I one day look at the glowing garden and pick the flower that's free
Look on as I pluck its pedals
And wonder what nature may bring to me?

In the midst of all the madness,
Of the chaos and the loss,
Will I ever be one to turn a blind eye
To the ones who were unable to cross?
On the bridge, through the leaves,
 Searching for love from thee?
Will I ever be able
To go back to where I belong,
To live life properly?

Secrets.
Secrets got that guy who lived down the road to kill himself.
Secrets.
Secrets can be dangerous.
Secrets.
Secrets can kill the hearts of those who you love but they still remain the same.
Some people are too scared of the consequences
Of coming clean and admitting to the truth.
Emotionally unstable
Emotionally unable
To speak
About
My secrets.

She stared at the mirror, looking at her reflection.
Finally, she got to stare at the glass,
It became a habit,
And soon,
An obsession.
To look and stare at this possession.
To notice every flaw, fault, and mistake in her appearance.

•

There were not many mirrors in her home, just some in the washroom.
So she went to the store, bought one, and hung it up in her room.
"Beautiful!" She thought to herself.
She watched the way her lips moved as she caressed her reflection.

•

Sometimes on these types of objects there's a sign that reads:
Warning objects in mirror may be closer than they appear.
Yet there's no warning that tells us that pupils in the mirror may be more beautiful than they appear.
There are so many warning signals,
So why are there are none for this device?
Because that girl stared into the mirror for hours on end,
And what she once called beauty had turned to flaw by the time that she went to bed.
It was a form of self harm, just not too visible is all
So it caused no alarm,

The loss of weight and gain of clear skin.
She started to get compliments like
"Damn girl, you thin!"
But they were shallow and completely
overlooked the beauty from within.

•

One day the girl taught the others how to
'look good'.
She grabbed a few mirrors and laid them
against the wall,
They all sat in a line,
"Now point out a flaw!"
The girls sat there nearly sobbing as they
realized what she had done;
She was trying to kill their minds,
One by one.
They snapped out of their reflective stares
and looked each other in the eyes,
They said, "You are beautiful, don't let the
mirror feed you its lies."

Visible beauty can be a disease,
A disguise.
Some people think it's all that matters
Because when they think of beauty, what truly comes to mind?
Is it kindness and generosity?
No.
It is the looks of their dream partner,
Or their dream selves.

In reality, true beauty is overlooked
Because true beauty is not seen but rather felt.
It is not simply an attribute,
But an entire ocean
With depths waiting to be explored.
Where only 5% has been seen by our eyes,
But we know that the remaining 95% holds more.
More mystery,
More beauty,
More comedy,
More art,
More love,
More.

Is this destiny?
Is this fate?
Is being here all a part of my mistake?
Am I dead,
Or am I still breathing?
Is the world around me still weaving
The strings of knowledge and the strings of the unknown,
Pulling each thread to bring humanity closer to its throne?
Is this fate or is it by pure choice?
Is our lack of humanity taken or have we thrown it away?
Have we decided to ruin ourselves day by day?
Or are we simply going through the motions of this endless cycle?
Emotionless wrecks on motorcycles.
We think we own this place so much
Greed and power take over us
Sin disguising itself in every which way
People are killing themselves every single day
And I still wonder
If it's by fate or pure choice
That humanity has lost its meaning
And we simply watch from the windows of our Rolls Royce.
I wonder if we could ever all possibly care
And attempt to change what is truly unfair.
But then I remind myself that maybe it's just not our destiny

Because sometimes the people with the threads are the ones who quite simply write history.

Loud no's couldn't stop you
Maybe sad yes's would make it all better?

Society needs to wake the hell up
Because
There are little girls who are being sexualised every day
Teenage bodies are touched and caressed by old men in every which way
Little boys are being raped by people wearing robes
Using their "holiness" as a way to be protected from their sins
And not to mention the misogyny that we simply allow to exist
Not only within our own families and communities but within our politics too
Where men who can't even name the different parts of the female reproductive system are passing laws to control their bodies.
Society needs to wake the hell up
Because I'm tired of being scared as I go on early morning runs
Society needs to wake the hell up because kids shouldn't be put into concentration camps and neither should Muslims in 2019
We need to wake up because oppression isn't the key to a better world
And because if we don't we are all bound to go extinct.
So I don't know how many times it must be said that we need to wake the hell up
Because if we do not than society will be stuck in a world
Where little children are over sexualized,
Where men are unable to cry,
Where humans are left to die.

Part 2

Rain helps flowers blossom

Humanity.

I am a human,
Flaws is my middle name.
I have told too many lies,
And hidden too many truths.
I am corrupted by what I know,
Yet hurt by what I don't.

I am a human with a sword at my throat.
With the crowds waiting to hear what I'll say
But when I slip up, will they boo in dismay?
I am scared,
I fear for my life everyday.

I am a child
Whose voice is talked over.
Whose ideas are crushed,
And whose singing is hushed.

We are the children,
Pure and strong,
The adults fear our reign,
Because we know where we belong.
We are the children,
The future of our people.
Oh society please treat us well,
We are simply the people's people.

I have a task for you
It's a really simple thing to do.
I want you to go outside
And I want you to breathe
I want you to list 7 things you can see
1.
2.
3.
4.
5.
6.
7.
5 things you can touch
1.
2.
3.
4.
5.
3 you can hear
1.
2.
3.
2 you can smell
1.
2.
And 1 you can love
1.
I now want you to ponder about all of the above.
I want you to wonder why everything was created.
I want you to open up your mind
And I want you to explore
I want you to live freely

And to live freely is to implore.
I want you to be protected
But I also want you to be wide awake;
To see the crisis we are facing
And everything that is at stake.
I want you to breathe in the fresh air
And understand that it is not
Something we will always live with
If we remain so distraught.
We need to learn
And we need to grow
This all starts in these beautiful fields
Which seem simple but are beautifully complicated.
I want you to come outside every single day
I want you to breathe.
I want you to play.
I want you to regain the childhood that you never had.
I want you to not be a boring adult.
I want you to loosen up.
I want you to be happy and to fly high on the swings in the park.
I want you to understand what this world is
And what it is not.
I want you to live
And to feel
And to accept your reality
Because it is a bittersweet thing that we must accept;
That we must stay strong to fight for or against.
Live, love, laugh
It's a simple task.

A woman's value
They say
Is determined based on how much she can do
How well she can cook
How beautiful she is
How well she can do it.
A woman's value
Is something unique
They say
It's found when
She's quiet
And calm
And agreeable.

They say a woman worth value is
Hard to come by
They say
A woman's value
Is as thick her thighs
But a woman's value is
Quickly taken away
When a woman shows some skin
For one day
And so they use it to
Abuse
A woman's value.

So, Here's the truth about a woman's value:

A woman's value
Is found everyday
Whether she can get out of bed or not
Whether she's smart or not
Whether she can cook or not
Whether she can clean or not
Whether she's outspoken
Or just a shy queen
A woman's value
Should not be mistaken
Because a woman
Oh yes, a woman
Has value
As soon as she's born
And it does not change based on societal norms.

I have zits and so do you
We're teens—it's nothing new.
She has cellulite but it also affects 80% of all women.
He may be short but he's just trying to live.

She may be old
And her voice may be low
But sit down and listen;
Open your ears,
Close your throat.
Sit and listen to her fables and stories
Because she has lived a long life with memories that need to be shared.

That man who can't walk lost his legs in the war
And that homeless guy over there that you are claiming is lazy
Looks for a job on the daily.
You know that girl who you called a slut?
She was raped by a man whom she knew and she trusted
She was raped by a man who she referred to as her older cousin.
Remember those immigrants you told to go back to their own country?
Every day they want to but there's nothing to go back to
Other than crushed walls and guns and barricades and war.
They were refugees but they were brown so you refused to implore
About how it would feel to be in their place.

In judging any of these people you are
acting like a disgrace
I want you to get off of your high horse
And go and apologize.
I want you to make the world a better place.
I want you to stop judging people as if you
know everything about them.
I want you to look at people with curiosity
and wonder
Not with eyes of destruction
And with eyes of cruelty.
I want for all of our hearts to be pure;
I want us to regain our lost humanity.

I've **learned** that with great knowledge
Comes great responsibility
Because with great knowledge
You begin to lose faith in humanity.
Knowledge has a price
That is stolen from all
But only some are able to realize what they no longer have
In this prison called life
Only some can really see
Our dark,
Harsh,
And true reality.
So only some can see the price all of us have paid
At one point of our lives
We paid the taxes
On our lives
Sold ourselves
For a little extra money
Tell me now
If the price you've paid has left you satisfied?
You paid with your happiness
Has your success given you more joy?

Live and be in the moment
And this will be a step to a good life
For always dwelling on the past
And searching for a future that may never even exist is a complete waste of time.

I shall not hate for it's not my fate.
I will love and prosper.
Like a flower, my stem will sprout from a seed,
And good morals will be the water that nourishes me.
The sunshine will be like my mind: bright and free,
I will have ideas flowing from leaf to leaf.
And negativity being nothing more than an insect that flies away.
I will grow tall as a sunflower,
My kindness will carry me;
My stem will be my faith,
Keeping me in place,
Holding me firm and tall.
I will no longer be small,
Easily stepped on and hurt.
I will chase my dreams and I will go as far as the wind will carry my seeds.
I shall not hate, it's just not in me.

Hope

I've been left broken,
Once again.
It's as if I'm stranded on an island with no escape.
There are other people
And there are other boats,
but no one is willing to help.
Is it possible to feel as though
You are in complete isolation,
While around hundreds of people?
While in front of a crowd?
While in a classroom where everyone laughs and talks?
While at a party where everyone is dancing?
Why has my isolation broken me?
Try being the odd one out in a group of three,
Try being the one that's bullied;
The one that's outcasted
And whose life is filled with torment.
You've probably been there,
Now it's time to look up,
To accept the pain and loss
And to show your true self.
To spread your wings that glow ever so bright.
So try new things,
To find your delight.
To speak up, even if you haven't been spoken to,
Because out of all of the people,
It Starts
With
 You.

Although I can't really get it all out of my head
I know that one day it won't creep up at me while I'm in bed
And one day I'll be healed
And my thoughts won't be so heavily holding me down
One day my life will change
And I'm willing to wait
For all of the hurt
And for all of the pain to finally wash away.

Every problem can be fixed.
I know at one point your pure soul was tricked.
You slipped up in the game, cheated, and won.
You slipped up but it was still fun.
But in the process of fun you lost it all,
You fell in too deep, and dug your own hole.
Your eyes rained
But the tears can still produce flowers too.
Because without rain, the soil will dry,
The canvas will be blank,
No story will be alive.
Every problem can be fixed,
Even if there is a bit of dismay,
Finding peace in the chaos should be your goal for today.

I know it makes no sense to you right now:
The pain
The sorrow
The sadness
The loneliness.
I know that you're trying so hard to get out
of bed every morning
And I know you are trying to get back on
your feet
And I know that nothing you do seems to
feel right
And you feel lost,
You feel Scared
And you feel Sad,
But one day
You'll look back at these hardships and you
will understand.
You will understand that missing that bus
on Monday morning doesn't really matter
now
And that her betrayal has only made you
stronger.
One day you'll be strong enough to see
through the hurt and the agony
And you'll see a light that has been dimmed
over the years.
You will brighten it with kindness,
Gratitude,
As well as empathy.
You will understand that everything
happened for a reason
And that these trials will never end as long
as we walk down these streets,
As long as we stand,

And as long as we breathe.
One day you will come to terms with it
And you'll find it.
You'll finally find
Your inner peace.

I thought that
I'd never feel happy
Because I thought that everything has a price.
I thought that I'd always be left all alone
With no place to go,
No people to call home.
And so my thoughts were the reason of my despair
But one day I decided that this self torture is simply not fair
And so I woke up that day
And I decided to change
I decided that I will begin to have a say
In who I am
And in who I will become.
I finally decided that I will be happy
Because being sad is tiring
And it is a waste of time
From now on I'm going to look at the bright side of life;
My, is it ever divine.

Her smile could light the sky for days,
Her teeth shone like pearls.
Her eyes were gemstones.
Hair covered with silk,
Skin glowing like a gold coin,
A summer day's simple rejoice.
An open book yet a closed door;
Only open to those who'd implore.
She was wide awake in mid-day,
But at night was when she was truly alive.
When her soul relished in the moonlight
And the wind blew against her skin as she drove out of sight.
She drove through darkness and into the light,
The dawn of a new day had just arrived.
A new day, with a new horizon with new steps to be taken and new paths to be explored.
Her gemstone eyes gazed at the morning sky,
She fell asleep feeling invincible,
May her soul never die.

Love

I need this to stop
So if there's something really going on
Just tell me.
Write me a note, it doesn't have to be long.
Slip it under my door while I play our song.
Tell me how you truly feel,
Is it only I who feels this ethereal?
I think there's something going on here
But until you let me know
I'll need this to stop,
To simply be able
To live my life fully

And to finally be stable.

I'm not in love with him
But in some galaxy,
In some far away land
I've found it
And I am in love.

I am not in love with some simple-minded boy,
Who enjoys using girls as his toy,
I am in love with the ocean, with the sea
With the tangles in our hair when we begin to sleep
How the moon creeps over us
As we weep.

I am in love
With God.
With what he has created.
With the universe as it has escalated
And I see reality so vividly
Because my reality begins to feel like a dream.
My nightmares are short
And my dreams outweigh them
So, when you ask "are you in love?"
I will simply say "Yes. Yes I am" because it is the honest truth
I am in love
With a galaxy
Named
Me.

Some days I think things may have changed,
May have been different if I had stayed.
But then I remind myself of your cruel touch.
Your manipulative grin,
Your constant need to win.
I remind myself of these things
And guilt, I no longer feel.
For if I had stayed, I would have never blossomed into something so ethereal.

When I look up at the stars
I try to forget
Your curly hair
And your beautiful skin
Your laugh
And rosy cheeks
Your sweet demeanour
And a love that was clean.
It may have been short
Because you live halfway across the country but
If I met you again
I think we'd still have an instant connection
I think that we would be so in love
And that we'd make silly jokes
And live
And laugh so damn much together.
I want that, and I'm going to wait for that to come back to me.

Love saves
Yet you're still scared of it.
Love creates
Yet you still shelter yourself from it.
Love is brave
But you hide from it like a coward behind closed doors.
Love exists
Yet you deny its very existence,
Because you fear being hurt
And being left all alone.
You fear someone building you up and then crushing you with your very own throne.
Love does not kill,
Fear, hatred, and a lack of it does.
Love is beautiful;
I wish it unto everyone.

Love is a word that is so overused.
It is so beautiful, yet so abused.
What comes to mind when you think of this word?
Is it a warm cup of hot cocoa shared with the one you love?
Or is it discord and turmoil,
Tears and agony?
To me, it's all of the above.
When you sign up for love, you aren't signing up for perfection.
You're signing up for another human.
For someone with fears,
Anger,
And a voice.
For someone with emotions, like you.
For someone slightly new.
For one that is unique;
Special in their own little way.
For love may have tears but there's still hot cocoa on the way.

Joy

I'm watching as the waves hit the shore
In a ferocious line
Their collision with the sand makes a noise as loud as a lion
Beams of the sun hit my face
Drying the rain,
Clouds begin to leave;
It's finally a clear day.
I finally begin to feel
Something I no longer thought I could:
Joy.

The flowers of joy begin to bloom,
Although scars from the windy day in April remain,
Its petals are still apparent,
Graceful and smooth.

Sad memories may still be there
But her happy thoughts overtake the negativity.
Rather than letting her sadness overtake her happiness,
She chooses the road of optimism to soothe what is there.
She once hid her despair, but now wears it as a proud token of what can be there.
Of what can happen
Of where she can be
Of the happiness in life that finally cradles her to sleep.

To be raw
And to share the most honest truth
To be in the moment
To be in tune.
To not overthink
But to live and to breathe,
To simply experience
And to disassemble the leaves.
To keep your head held high
With tears strolling down your face,
To overlook the labels

Is to live in grace.

Look at the trees,
The flicker of their leaves.
The wind,
Feel it flutter against your skin.
Lose yourself in the beauty,
That of both around you, and within.

You say you seek happiness
And you say you seek love.
You say you feel unwanted and you wish
someone was there to simply give you a
hug.
But you forget everyday
That you lose your mind
Over the simple things that could bring you
joy
Because you're too busy being blind.
Blinded by sadness
And the feeling of loss
Of loneliness
Of disgust
Of being annoying
Or not cool enough.
And so everyday
You complain and you complain
And you destroy yourself;
You destroy your mind
Because you think the world hates you,
You think that the world is out to get you.
You think that you're not good enough.
When in fact,
The world hates none.
But that doesn't mean the world is easy;
The world is difficult.
It's filled with tests and battles.
It's filled with sad goodbyes and worthless
helloes.
It's filled with beautiful lies and filthy
truths.
It's composed of madness
And it feeds off of us

Off of our souls.
The world is like a body,
If you give it healthy food it will flourish
But all we do is give it unhealthy food
We give the world a negative attitude.
A dark approach;
A slender goodbye.
The inability to be patient and accept that
the world will give us something better than
what we had, all in good time.
If we are willing to be patient
And if we are willing to say goodbye
To our terrible attitudes that don't make the
world a better place;
That simply dig a hole deeper and deeper
into this planet
That will one day be our graves.
Only then will we be able to be happy and
filled with joy
Because you will never feel those emotions
if you're stuck in your own rut.

We are our own worst enemies
And we are always looking for friends
But you can't ever be content unless you are
willing to accept
That loss can be painful
But it can be beautiful too
In the end
Only you can decide
If the glass is half empty
Or if the glass is half full.

The rain has reinvented us in so many different ways

Because if the sun was always out it would burn us out.

The pain that the rain has brought

Along with the loneliness

And the societal diseases

Has brought so much agony

But they have also brought so many lessons to be learned

And new paths to be explored.

If the rain did not exist in our lives

Than we would have no real sense of joy

Because we would constantly be ungrateful.

We would not ever regain any sense of our humanity.

We would be blind in looking at the destruction of the world.

We think that the rain is here because it is out to get us

But

We forget that life was never meant to be easy,

It is a test.

We must not dwell on the pain from the rain

Because the sun will shine when we are drained.

The glimpses of the sun's rays may not always be visible to you

But they will come in good time

Just be sure to wait

And to be patient

Because for you, my dear, a whole story filled with love, laughs,

and joy has been written

Uniquely to best fit

What must be there

For you to be happy

And for you to rejoice over your life.

For you there are oceans of words

And the rain adds into these stories

Creating the best of what sorrows have gone unheard.

So, never lose hope

And never forget that you may be sad now

But the rain reinvents all

And the sun leaves none behind

We must grow from the rain

Because without growth we will be stuck in constant sadness and loss

But in order to learn and grow

Never forget the fact that the rain needed to pour on you

And that the sun has come to dry you off.

Sometimes you are so caught up in your own pain

And so you begin to overlook the beauty that exists

You overlook the joy and you cover it up with sadness.

The rain can help reinvent you, but it is only a part of the massive puzzle that exists.

You need to move forward and learn from the rain

Because the rain has written a message that ends with your name.

Acknowledgements

I would like to acknowledge my supportive parents. I would like to thank River Straza for illustrating the cover page. I would also like to thank my grandparents (and great-grandparents) who never fail to teach me something new. I want to acknowledge all of my family members. I would like to thank all of my friends and just anyone who has ever helped me. I also want to thank everyone and every instance that has ever hurt me because it has changed and shaped me as a person.

About the Author

Huda Abdelkerim is a Canadian author that was born in 2004 and was raised in Regina, Saskatchewan. She has also lived in her father's home country, Tunisia, on multiple occasions. She is a national debater who has attended junior nationals for 3 years in a row. She enjoys speaking about social justice and having deep conversations with her friends, but if she feels as though she cannot explain something directly to other people, she will write it down instead. Huda enjoys going on long drives as well as being surrounded by nature.

Made in the USA
Columbia, SC
14 March 2021